Knock Knock Jokes

Joe King

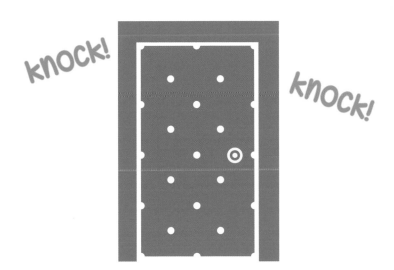

Abdo Kids Junior
is an Imprint of Abdo Kids
abdobooks.com

Abdo
ABDO KIDS JOKES
Kids

abdobooks.com

Published by Abdo Kids, a division of ABDO, P.O. Box 398166, Minneapolis, Minnesota 55439.
Copyright © 2022 by Abdo Consulting Group, Inc. International copyrights reserved in all countries.
No part of this book may be reproduced in any form without written permission from the publisher.
Abdo Kids Junior™ is a trademark and logo of Abdo Kids.

Printed in the United States of America, North Mankato, Minnesota.

102021

012022

 THIS BOOK CONTAINS
RECYCLED MATERIALS

Photo Credits: Getty Images, Shutterstock

Production Contributors: Teddy Borth, Jennie Forsberg, Grace Hansen

Design Contributors: Candice Keimig, Pakou Moua

Library of Congress Control Number: 2021940304

Publisher's Cataloging-in-Publication Data

Names: King, Joe, author.

Title: Knock knock jokes / by Joe King

Description: Minneapolis, Minnesota : Abdo Kids, 2022 | Series: Abdo kids jokes | Includes online resource.

Identifiers: ISBN 9781098209186 (lib. bdg.) | ISBN 9781644946329 (pbk.) | ISBN 9781098209889 (ebook)
    | ISBN 9781098260248 (Read-to-Me ebook)

Subjects: LCSH: Jokes--Juvenile literature. | Wit and humor--Juvenile literature. | Knock-knock jokes--
    Juvenile literature.

Classification: DDC 818.602--dc23

Table of Contents

Knock Knock Jokes

Knock, knock.

Who's there?

Kanga.

Kanga who?

Actually, it's kanga*roo*.

MOOOOO!

Knock, knock.
    Who's there?
Cows say.
    Cows say who?
No silly, cows say moo!

Knock, knock.

Who's there?

Spell.

Spell who?

W-H-O!

Knock, knock.
Who's there?
Owls.
Owls say who?
Yes, they do!

7

Knock, knock.

Who's there?

Boo.

Boo who?

What're you cryin' about?!

Knock, knock.

Who's there?

A little old lady.

A little old lady who?

I didn't know you could yodel!

9

Knock, knock.

Who's there?

Water.

Water who?

Water you asking so many questions for? *Open up*!

MHMM!

HA!

HA!

Knock, knock.

Who's there?

Mustache.

Mustache who?

Mustache you a question, but I'll *shave* it for later!

11

Knock, knock.

Who's there?

Amish.

Amish who?

Really? You don't look like a shoe!

Knock, knock.

Who's there?

Radio.

Radio who?

Radio not, here I come!

13

Knock, knock.

Who's there?

Justin.

Justin who?

Justin the neighborhood and thought I'd stop by!

LOL!

WHEW!

Knock, knock.
   Who's there?
Anita.
   Anita who?
Anita glass of water.
It's hot out here!

15

Knock, knock.

Who's there?

Harry.

Harry who?

Harry up and let me in!

Knock, knock.

Who's there?

Dewey.

Dewey who?

Dewey have to keep telling jokes?

Knock, knock.

Who's there?

Shore.

Shore who?

Shore hope you loved all these jokes!

Taco 'bout hilarious!

LETTUCE LAUGH!

YUM!

Knock, knock.

Who's there?

Taco.

Taco who?

Taco to you later! You're taking too long to open the door.

Joke-Telling Tips!

- Know your audience

- Timing is everything

- Confidence is key

- Go out on a high note!

Glossary

Dewey
referring to the Dewey Decimal System, a system used by libraries to organize books into groups. Each title has its own Dewey number.

pun
a joke using a word that sounds like a different word or has another meaning. Examples from this book are "Dewey" (Do we) and "Anita" (I need a).

Index

Abdo Kids ONLINE
FREE! ONLINE MULTIMEDIA RESOURCES

Visit **abdokids.com** to access crafts, games, videos, and more!

Use Abdo Kids code

AKK9186

or scan this QR code!